This journal belongs to:

Made in the USA
Monee, IL
12 March 2022

92782459R00063